EARTH IN ACTION

AVALANCHES

by Wendy Lanier

Content Consultant
Jennifer Rivers Cole, PhD
Department of Earth & Planetary Sciences
Harvard University

CORE
LIBRARY

Published by ABDO Publishing Company, PO Box 398166, Minneapolis, MN 55439. Copyright © 2014 by Abdo Consulting Group, Inc. International copyrights reserved in all countries. No part of this book may be reproduced in any form without written permission from the publisher. The Core Library™ is a trademark and logo of ABDO Publishing Company.

Printed in the United States of America,
North Mankato, Minnesota
052013
092013

♻ THIS BOOK CONTAINS AT LEAST 10% RECYCLED MATERIALS.

Editor: Mirella Maxwell
Series Designer: Becky Daum

Library of Congress Control Number: 2013932149

Cataloging-in-Publication Data
Lanier, Wendy.
 Avalanches / Wendy Lanier.
   p. cm. -- (Earth in action)
ISBN 978-1-61783-936-8 (lib. bdg.)
ISBN 978-1-62403-001-7 (pbk.)
1. Avalanches--Juvenile literature. 2. Natural disasters--Juvenile literature.
I. Title.
551.57--dc23

                                              2013932149

CONTENTS

CHAPTER ONE

IN THE LINE OF FIRE

Cold temperatures and snow are normal winter weather in Alaska. But January 2000 produced the heaviest snowfall the small fishing port of Cordova had ever seen. The nearby group of mountains, Heney Range, could not be seen most of January. Near the top was a bowl-shaped area the size of a stadium. The bowl had been collecting snow

The small fishing port of Cordova, Alaska, is used to winter weather and avalanches. But they were not prepared for the January 2000 avalanche.

throughout January. Now it was snowing hard again on the morning of January 26.

Danger Overhead

Jerry LeMaster lived in a Cordova neighborhood known as 5.5 Mile. On January 26, the heater in LeMaster's home was not working. LeMaster had to go to the detached garage for firewood. He pulled on warm clothes, grabbed a shovel, and headed outside. The 50-mile-per-hour (80-km/h) wind created whiteout conditions. LeMaster had a hard time seeing.

After gathering firewood for a while, LeMaster heard a distant rumbling. It sounded like thunder. He glanced up at Heney Range and saw a cloud of snow rolling downward. LeMaster was not alarmed. He had seen avalanches in Cordova before. But they hardly ever came close to his house. Still, it seemed best to seek shelter in the house. The distant thunder quickly became a roaring noise. LeMaster turned to see a wall flying in his direction, as he was ready to head upstairs. The rest of his home exploded in the next few seconds. His longtime companion, Martha, was not able to escape the blast. Rescuers found her body in her favorite chair several hours later.

Buried Alive

Members of the local fire department searched for LeMaster for five hours after the avalanche. He also volunteered for the local fire department, which meant he carried a pager. Every few minutes the rescuers stopped to page him and listened quietly. Finally a rescuer heard LeMaster yelling.

The group began to dig in excitement as they pulled away scraps of the house. They dug through a 15-foot (5-m) layer of thick snow and broken trees. Avalanche expert Jill Fredston warned the

The Deadliest Avalanche in US History

A late February 1910 snowstorm stranded two Great Northern Railroad trains in Wellington, Washington. The trains waited six days for help. Just after midnight on March 1, 1910, both trains were swept off the tracks by a 14-foot (4-m) wall of snow. Ninety-six people died.

Homes, buildings, and cars in Cordova, Alaska, were covered when the Heney Range avalanche came speeding down the mountain in January 2000.

group to slow down. Moving too quickly might cause the air space around LeMaster to cave in.

After another 15 minutes of digging, the rescuers were able to see LeMaster. There was a furnace beside him, holding up a blue door. The door held up a beam. LeMaster's legs were caught in parts of a wall. The tangle of the furnace, the door, and the beam created an air pocket around his head. It was enough to keep him alive.

Rescuers continued to work slowly and carefully until LeMaster stopped breathing. Then rescuers quickly pulled him to safety and got him to the hospital. He had been trapped nearly six hours. LeMaster recovered from his injuries.

Cordova: In the News Again

Cordova has seen several avalanches since January 2000. An avalanche covered the Copper River Highway for more than six hours in April 2012. This created a serious threat since the only way in or out of Cordova is by air or boat. Fortunately, there were no injuries in this avalanche.

A man assesses the damage of the January 2000 avalanche in Cordova.

New Respect for Avalanche Danger

The January 2000 Cordova avalanche destroyed four homes and two warehouses. Several other homes were damaged. The half-mile (800-m) wide path of the avalanche created a mess. The mix of trees, buildings, and snow was 20 feet (6 m) deep in places. The avalanche also blocked more than 1,000 feet (305 m) of Copper River Highway. This is the only road to the airport. Property damage in Cordova totaled more than $11 million. Cordova no longer allows houses to be built in the 5.5 Mile neighborhood. This neighborhood is now an avalanche danger zone.

After the January 2000 Cordova avalanche, the *Anchorage Daily News* printed an accident report on Jerry LeMaster's rescue:

> *Thursday, January 27, 2000 - Five hours after an avalanche roared down a Cordova slope. . . dozens of rescuers were still digging Wednesday afternoon through the debris covering the home of Jerry LeMaster. It had been two hours since the body of LeMaster's companion, Martha Quales, had been pulled out. LeMaster was still missing. . . rescuers tried paging [LeMaster] to make his beeper sound. Every so often they'd order all cell phones, radios and backhoe engines silenced so they could listen. They were holding another paging test at 2:55 p.m. when they first heard him.*
>
> Source: Liz Ruskin, Peter Porco, and Natalie Phillips. "Rescuers Save Cordova Man after Avalanche." Anchorage Daily News January 27, 2000. Web. Accessed February 26, 2013.

Consider Your Audience

Review the accident report closely. How could you change it for a different audience, such as your parents or friends? Write a blog post conveying this same information for the new audience. What is the best way to get your point across?

CHAPTER TWO

ANATOMY OF AN AVALANCHE

An avalanche is a powerful mass of snow resulting from the pull of gravity down a hill or mountain slope. The snow mixes with trees, rocks, and parts of buildings as it tumbles downward. An avalanche can move up to 300,000 cubic yards (230,000 cubic meters) of snow. That is equal to 20 football fields covered in 10 feet (3 m) of snow!

An avalanche becomes more forceful as it races down a mountain, gathering speed and mixing with anything in its path.

Causes of Avalanches

The shape of the land, the weather, and the condition of the snow create the ingredients for an avalanche. An avalanche can occur on any slope angled between 25 and 60 degrees. Most avalanches occur on slopes between 35 and 45 degrees. The average staircase is 30 degrees.

A rise in temperature weakens the bond that holds snow together. Colder temperatures increase the weakness and tighten a snow slab. Changes in temperature and other weather conditions can change the stability of snow in just a few hours.

Avalanches are most common in the 24 hours during and after a snowstorm. When 12 or more inches of fresh snow cover an area, the new

The Beast Above

A long time ago, people used to think that avalanches were living creatures. Ancient Europeans told stories about the dragons and monsters that lived in the mountains. Sometimes they tried to scare them away by ringing church bells.

Human activity can start an avalanche.

snow can burden the main snowpack. Strong winds also increase the chance of an avalanche occurring. Footsteps, loud noises, and other human actions can also start an avalanche. All of these factors cause a weak layer below a snow slab to break.

Zones of an Avalanche

An avalanche has three zones. The starting zone is the point where unstable snow breaks and slides downward. Starting points are usually above the tree

Starting Zone

Track

Runout Zone

Debris

Anatomy of a Slab Avalanche

This figure shows the structure of a slab avalanche. After reading about avalanches, what did you imagine each part looked like? How has that idea changed? How does seeing this figure help you better understand each part of a slab avalanche?

line and near the ridge of the mountain. However, starting points can appear at any point along the slope.

The avalanche track is the path an avalanche follows down a slope. A strip of missing trees indicates an avalanche track. Piles of snow and debris at the bottom of a slope are also indications of an avalanche track.

The runout zone is where the snow and debris come to a stop. The snow in this area is thick, like concrete.

Types of Avalanches

There are different types of avalanches. The least dangerous avalanche is called a powder avalanche. A powder avalanche is made of loose, powdery snow. Powder avalanches usually cause little damage. But they do occasionally flatten buildings.

A slab avalanche is the most dangerous type of avalanche. A weak point deep within a snowpack causes it. Slab avalanches usually occur on the leeward side of a slope. A leeward side of a slope is the side of the slope the wind does not blow on. Once a slab

The Power of Snow

A fully developed avalanche can involve up to one million tons (1.02 million metric tons) of snow. The wind ahead of an avalanche can reach more than 200 miles per hour (320 km/h). These winds cause damage beyond the runout zone.

This slab avalanche was triggered by a skier. Slab avalanches are the most dangerous type.

avalanche is separated by gravity, the snow breaks loose. A slab of snow can travel at speeds up to 200 miles per hour (322 km/h).

The third type of avalanche is called a wet avalanche. A wet avalanche occurs when warmer temperatures melt snow layers on the surface of a snowpack. The upper layers melt. This weakens the bond between the layers of snow. The heavy top layer breaks free. Then it slides down a slope at speeds of 10 to 20 miles per hour (15 to 30 km/h).

EXPLORE ONLINE

The focus in Chapter Two was on the parts of an avalanche. It also discussed the causes of an avalanche. The Web site below focuses on the same subjects. As you know, every source is different. How is the information given on the Web site different from the information in this chapter? What information is the same? How do the two sources present information differently? What can you learn from this Web site?

Unleash an Avalanche
www.mycorelibrary.com/avalanches

CHAPTER THREE

WHERE IN THE WORLD?

Each year there are thousands of reported avalanches in the United States alone. Experts estimate thousands more avalanches occur where no one sees them.

The avalanches that grab attention are those affecting people. The number of people participating in winter sports has increased since the 1950s. This also increases the likelihood of avalanche accidents.

Mount Rainier in Washington has a history of large debris avalanches.

Avalanches across the World

Approximately 150 people are killed worldwide in avalanches each year. Hundreds more are hurt or trapped by sliding snow. According to the American Avalanche Association, most avalanches in the United States occur in January, February, and March. An average of 29 people die in avalanches each year in the United States.

France, Austria, Switzerland, and Italy encounter the greatest number of avalanches. These countries also have the greatest number of avalanche deaths each year. Hundreds of towns dot the mountainsides of the Alps. The mix of people and snow-covered

Avalanches Break Gold Rush Fever

During the late 1800s, thousands of people went to Alaska in search of gold. On April 3, 1898, five avalanches fell on hundreds of people climbing the Chilkoot Trail with their supplies. Historians believe more than 65 people might have died in the avalanches.

French rescue workers head out to search for the climbers buried in the July 2012 avalanche on Mont Maudit.

mountains creates many opportunities for avalanche accidents.

In July 2012, a group of 28 climbers were climbing Mont Maudit in the French Alps. The climbers had reached approximately 13,000 feet (3,900 m) when they were suddenly caught in an avalanche. Nine people were killed. The avalanche was likely caused by the footsteps of one of the climbers. Research shows a human starts a snow slide in 90 to 95 percent of avalanche accidents.

CHAPTER FOUR

AVALANCHE FORECASTING

The increase in avalanche accidents in recent years has created a new job in avalanche forecasting. Avalanche forecasters work in the mountains. They ski and ride snowmobiles to different areas of the mountain to check on snowpack. They provide a valuable public service making roadways and winter play areas safe for the public.

Avalanche forecasters around the world work hard to create safer mountain conditions.

Studying avalanches is dangerous and demanding work. There are few jobs available in this field, which makes the competition for a job high. Avalanche forecasters need a college degree in a science field. They also need experience in ski patrol and backcountry areas. Computer skills and making sense of information quickly is also important.

Another Day at the Office

Avalanche forecasters combine their knowledge of past avalanches with current information about land, weather, and snowpack conditions. This helps estimate where an avalanche may occur.

An avalanche forecaster usually spends two to three days per week in backcountry avalanche areas examining snowpack. A snow pit is a basic tool of avalanche forecasting. To create a snow pit, an avalanche forecaster digs out vertical pits on a slope. Each layer of snowpack is carefully observed and tested for stability.

Avalanche forecasters take time to teach avalanche safety and training classes. This helps more people be aware of unstable conditions.

Forecasters also spend time in the office looking over weather reports and avalanche data. Information gathered outside and in the office helps estimate the danger level on a slope. Avalanche forecasters often spend one day a week teaching avalanche safety classes.

Danger Levels

An avalanche forecaster can gather a lot of information. But there is still no way to know for

Avalanche Danger Scale

The North American Public Avalanche Danger Scale helps explain expected dangers in an area. The scale makes it easy for the public to understand the threat of possible avalanches. The scale also helps visitors to a mountain make informed decisions about visiting certain areas.

sure when an avalanche will happen. Avalanche forecasters issue warnings for areas when estimated danger levels get too high. They base warnings on the North American Public Avalanche Danger Scale. However, differences in snowpack and other conditions mean warnings can only apply to small areas. All of these factors make avalanche forecasting a difficult job.

Future of Forecasting

Researchers are looking for ways to make avalanche forecasting more exact. Swiss researchers are at the leading edge of this work. In Switzerland, 65 percent of the population lives in an area threatened by avalanches.

Danger Level	Symbol	Travel Advice	Likelihood of Avalanches	Avalanche Size and Distribution
5 Extreme		Avoid all avalanche terrain.	Certain	Large to very large avalanches in many areas.
4 High		Very dangerous avalanche conditions. Travel in avalanche terrain not recommended.	Very likely/ Likely	Large avalanches in many areas, or very large avalanches in specific areas.
3 Considerable		Dangerous avalanche conditions.	Likely/ Possible	Small avalanches in many areas, large avalanches in specific areas, or very large avalanches in isolated areas.
2 Moderate		Heightened avalanche conditions in specific areas.	Possible/ Unlikely	Small avalanches in specific areas or large avalanches in isolated areas.
1 Low		Generally safe avalanche conditions. Watch for unstable snow.	Unlikely	Small avalanches in isolated areas or extreme terrain.

North American Public Avalanche Danger Scale

This scale shows the danger levels that avalanche forecasters use when issuing warnings. Avalanche danger is determined by the likelihood, size, and distribution of avalanches.

Swiss researchers are working on computer programs to estimate the behavior of snow under different conditions. The programs gather information from a system of electronic monitors all over the

Computer programs help avalanche forecasters better predict the likelihood of an avalanche.

country. The information is fed into a central program and updated every 15 minutes. Avalanche forecasters use the information to estimate avalanche activity. Similar programs are being developed in the United States. The program is not perfect. It will still be at least ten years before avalanche forecasters stop using snow pits.

Jill Fredston and her husband are avalanche experts. They teach safety classes and serve as avalanche forecasters. Jill shares some of her feelings about their work in her book *Snowstruck*:

> *Still, we both chose to take on the cause of keeping people from getting killed in avalanches . . . [but, in spite of our efforts] new victims are born every year. We have taken on a problem that ultimately we cannot solve. . . . the sad reality is that even the best forecasting cannot prevent [accidents] . . . Some take comfort in knowing that the victims died 'doing what they loved to do,' but I have trouble getting past the reality that they needn't have died at all.*

Source: Jill Fredston. Snowstruck: In the Grip of Avalanches. Orlando: Harcourt, Inc., 2005. Print. 296–297.

Changing Minds

Jill Fredston's book, *Snowstruck*, discusses her work as an avalanche expert. She also talks about how avalanches are a problem that cannot be solved. Take a position on this belief. Imagine your best friend has the opposite opinion. Write a short essay trying to change your friend's mind. Make sure you state your opinion and your reasons for it. Include facts and details that support your reasons.

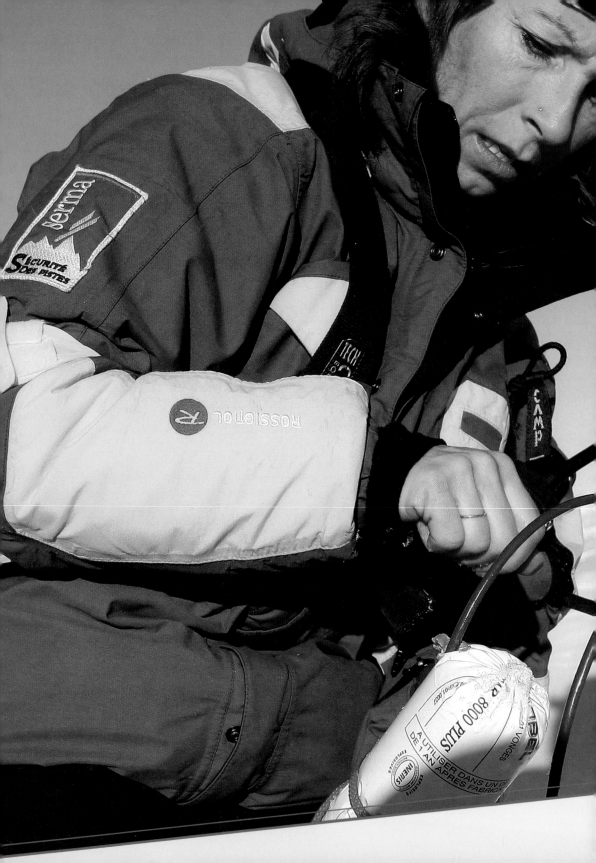

CHAPTER FIVE

LIVING WITH AVALANCHES

Snow does not avalanche until something starts its movement. Natural starters include changing weather and falling trees or ice. Ski patrols often use avalanche control to keep recreation areas safe. Avalanche control includes forecasting an area, using snow guards, and sometimes actively starting an avalanche. Ski patrols and avalanche forecasters decide if starting an avalanche will lessen the effect

Ski patrols start controlled avalanches to help lessen the damage a future avalanche can create.

Ski patrol members head out to search for buried avalanche victims. Many ski patrol teams work with trained dogs to help find the victims.

of a possible future, larger avalanche. The number of fatal avalanche accidents in controlled ski areas is less than 1 percent.

Most avalanche accidents happen outside recreation areas. Approximately 70 percent of the time, the avalanche occurs in an area known to the victims. Many avalanche victims are experienced snowmobilers, skiers, snowboarders, and climbers. Sometimes they know the danger but ignore it because they think they will be able to escape.

Common Sense Approach

The best defense against getting caught in an avalanche is common sense. Avoiding an avalanche is easier than getting out of one. Anyone who enjoys backcountry winter sports should know what to do in an avalanche. Safety courses from the National

What to Do If You're Caught in an Avalanche

If you are ever caught in an avalanche, here are a few tips to keep in mind:

- Try to get off the snow slab if you can.
- If you cannot get off the snow slab, grab a tree or rock.
- Use swimming motions to stay on top of the flow.
- As the avalanche slows down, clear air space in front of you to breathe. Try to get a hand above the snow to alert rescuers of your location.

It is important to always be aware of avalanche danger levels if you are near an avalanche-prone area.

Avalanche Center or other approved programs are a good place to start. These training sessions teach the basics of avalanche safety.

Having the right equipment is also important. Basic equipment for fun in the snow should include a shovel, an avalanche probe, and a rescue beacon. An avalanche probe is a pole used to find solid objects buried in snow. Rescue beacons let out a signal that allows an avalanche victim to be found sooner. At the start of every outing the beacon should be loaded with fresh batteries.

Today's technology lets you check the conditions on the slopes right from your phone. Free applications feature detailed avalanche conditions for more than 85 regions in North America. The information comes from avalanche centers throughout North America. This leaves no excuse for taking chances on the slopes.

Parks and resorts issue avalanche danger warning levels daily. It is

The Latest Avalanche Safety Equipment

Some of the latest avalanche safety technology includes AvaLungs and inflatable airbags and vest. An AvaLung is a device that lets an avalanche victim breathe into a mouthpiece. This mouthpiece carries the carbon dioxide the victim breathes out through a tube that runs behind his or her back. This keeps the victim from breathing the carbon dioxide in again. Inflatable airbags and vests work when the victim pulls a ripcord. The airbags or vests inflate around the victim. This helps keep the victim close to the surface of an avalanche flow.

New safety equipment, like the inflatable airbag, helps reduce the number of lives lost in avalanches.

important to check Web sites and avalanche hotlines daily for danger ratings.

No one should go into the backcountry without another person. Hollow-sounding snow and break lines in the snow are signals that an avalanche is about to happen. When in backcountry areas, stay on the lookout for signs of a possible avalanche.

Avalanche Rescue

An avalanche victim's best chance for survival is to be dug out of the snow within 15 minutes. A rescuer can move an area of snow the size of a household refrigerator with a shovel in approximately 10 minutes. Without a shovel, the process could take an hour. The victim may not survive.

Avalanches are both powerful and surprising. Knowledge, equipment, and fast action can mean the difference between life and death. No matter how many preparations are made, sometimes avalanches are unavoidable. The key is learning how to control the damage to property and lessen the danger to people.

Reducing Damage

Over the last few decades, scientists and researchers have looked for ways to reduce damage from an avalanche. The answers lie in three plans. One is changing the way the snow collects on the slopes. Another is reducing the size of the snow slab. The

In some areas, avalanche rakes are set up to keep snow in place. This helps prevent avalanches.

third plan is creating structures to divert snow to a runout zone away from people and buildings. In some areas, large, sturdy structures are built into the snowpack. Forests are replanted to serve as anchors. Special fences called avalanche rakes are built. These hold the snow in place and keep it from breaking. Dams and wedges are built at the base of slopes to divert avalanche runout away from populated areas. While these defensive measures are expensive, they are necessary to protect heavily populated areas.

Avalanches are a product of nature. It is unlikely we will ever be able to control them completely. But by studying the conditions and causes of avalanches it is possible we can find ways to live with them more safely. The more we study avalanches, the more we understand their immense power.

FURTHER EVIDENCE

Chapter Five covered safety tips and information about rescue. If you could pick out the main point of the chapter, what would it be? What evidence was given to support that point? Visit the Web site below to learn more about avalanche safety. Choose a quote from the Web site that relates to this chapter. Does this quote support the author's main point? Does it make a new point? Write a few sentences explaining how the quote you found relates to this chapter.

How to Survive an Avalanche
www.mycorelibrary.com/avalanches

TEN MAJOR AVALANCHES

September 4, 1618
Plurs, Switzerland

The Rodi Avalanche in Switzerland buried the town of Plurs on September 4, 1618. More than 2,400 lives were lost.

March 1, 1910
Wellington, Washington

In late February 1910, two trains waited in Wellington, Washington, for a snowstorm to pass through. Just after midnight on March 1, an avalanche swept both trains off the tracks. Ninety-six lives were lost.

December 13, 1916
Italian-Austrian Alps

Italy and Austria both had military bases in the Alps during World War I (1914–1918). Heavy snow caused more than one avalanche on December 13, 1916. The avalanches caused the deaths of 10,000 soldiers.

Winter 1950–1951
Swiss-Austrian Alps

The Swiss-Austrian Alps suffered a terrifying winter from 1950 to 1951. Heavy snowstorms caused more than 600 avalanches throughout the season. More than 265 lives were lost.

January 12, 1954
Blons, Austria

On the morning of January 12, an avalanche buried 118 people in Blons, Austria. As rescue workers tried to save the victims, a second avalanche swept through the town. The final death count was more than 200.

January 10, 1962
Ranrahircá, Peru

Mount Huascaran let go rock, snow, and mud onto the village of Ranrahircá in 1962. More than 2,700 people died, and nearly every home was destroyed.

May 31, 1970

Yungáy, Peru

The Great Peruvian Earthquake shook northern Peru in late May. This caused snow and ice to race down Mount Huascaran. The entire city was buried, resulting in approximately 20,000 lives lost.

March 1979

Lahaul Valley, India

Five days of snowstorms caused snow from the Himalayas to come racing down the mountains toward the Lahaul Valley below. Nearly 20 feet (6 m) of snow buried the valley. More than 200 lives were lost.

September 20, 2002

North Ossetia, Russia

A collapsed slab of snow on Mount Kazbek let go an avalanche that destroyed several villages in Russia. An estimated 140 lives were lost, including a production crew who were on a film set.

April 7, 2012

Siachen Glacier, Pakistan

An avalanche on April 7, 2012, hit a Pakistani military base in the Siachen Glacier region. More than 140 soldiers and civilians were buried under deep snow and died.

Why Do I Care?

This book discusses how avalanches have affected many people's lives. Even if you have never experienced an avalanche yourself, how do the victims' experiences connect to your life? Maybe you have been trapped somewhere, or maybe you have experienced another weather-related disaster. Write down two or three ways an avalanche victim's experiences connect to your life.

Take a Stand

The 5.5 Mile neighborhood was eventually zoned as an avalanche danger area. Take a position on turning neighborhoods into avalanche danger areas. Then write a short essay explaining your opinion. Make sure you give reasons for your opinion. Give some evidence to support those reasons.

Say What?

Learning about avalanches can mean learning a lot
of new vocabulary. Find five words in this book that
you've never heard or seen before. Find out what
these words mean. Using your own ideas, write down
the meaning of each word. Then use each word in a
sentence.

Tell the Tale

Chapter One discusses an avalanche in Cordova,
Alaska. Write 200 words that tell the true story of this
event. Be sure to set the scene, develop a sequence
of events, and offer a conclusion.

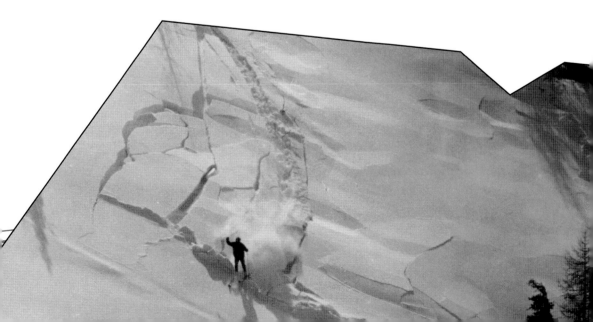

GLOSSARY

air pocket
a space that allows an avalanche victim to breathe when buried

avalanche probe
a collapsible 10- to 12-foot (3- to 3.7-m) pole for finding solid objects buried in snow

backcountry
sparsely populated areas outside the boundaries of designated winter sports areas

beacon
a radio transceiver that can send or search for a signal; part of avalanche safety gear

leeward
the side of the slope the wind does not blow on

particle
a relatively small portion of something

runout zone
the portion of an avalanche path where the debris typically comes to rest

slab
large section of thickly packed snow

snowpack
layers of snow that built up from one snowfall to another

whiteout
heavy snow with poor visibility

LEARN MORE

Books

Bishop, Amanda, and Vanessa Walker. *Avalanche and Landslide Alert!* New York: Crabtree, 2004.

Hamilton, John. *Avalanches.* Edina, MN: ABDO, 2006.

Hynes, Margaret. *Navigators: Extreme Weather.* New York: Kingfisher, 2011.

Web Links

To learn more about avalanches, visit ABDO Publishing Company online at **www.abdopublishing.com**. Web sites about avalanches are featured on our Book Links page. These links are routinely monitored and updated to provide the most current information available. Visit **www.mycorelibrary.com** for free additional tools for teachers and students.

INDEX

ABOUT THE AUTHOR

Wendy Lanier is an author, teacher, and speaker living in Beaumont, Texas. She writes and speaks on a variety of subjects. She and her husband of 25 years have three dogs, two daughters, and one granddaughter.